$\mathcal{S}$ EASONS $\mathcal{O}$ F $\mathcal{L}$ IFE

AUTUMN

—— A ——

TIME

—— TO ——

HARVEST

$\mathcal{M}$ EDITATIONS

Catharine Walkinshaw

A
JANET
THOMA
BOOK

Thomas Nelson Publishers
NASHVILLE

Published in Nashville, Tennessee, by Janet Thoma Books, a division of Thomas Nelson Publishers, Inc., and distributed in Canada by Word Communications, Ltd., Richmond, British Columbia, and in the United Kingdom by Word (UK), Ltd., Milton Keynes, England.

Library of Congress Cataloging-in-Publication Data

Walkinshaw, Catharine.
　　Autumn : a time to harvest / by Catharine Walkinshaw.
　　　　p.　　cm. — (Seasons of life meditations)
　　ISBN 0-8407-9279-4
　　1. Autumn—Religious aspects—Christianity—Meditations.
2. Devotional calendars. I. Title. II. Series.
BV4832.2.W335 1994
242'.2—dc20

93-8606
CIP

Printed in the United States of America
1 2 3 4 5 — 97 96 95 94

To everything there is a season,
  A time for every purpose under heaven:
  A time to be born,
    And a time to die;
  A time to plant,
    And a time to pluck what is planted;
  A time to kill,
    And a time to heal;
  A time to break down,
    And a time to build up;
  A time to weep,
    And a time to laugh;
  A time to mourn,
    And a time to dance;
  A time to cast away stones,
    And a time to gather stones;
  A time to embrace,
    And a time to refrain from embracing;
  A time to gain,
    And a time to lose;
  A time to keep,
    And a time to throw away;
  A time to tear,
    And a time to sew;
  A time to keep silence,
    And a time to speak;
  A time to love,
    And a time to hate;
  A time of war,
    And a time of peace.
                          Ecclesiastes 3:1–8

For Chuck and Debbie,
who showed me how
precious life is.

. . . .

To Everything There Is a Season

The seasons of life are more than spring, summer, fall, and winter. There is a season when you prepare for childbirth, and a season for saying goodbye to a loved one. There is the season of working hard for financial security, and there is the season of smelling roses and walking hand in hand with a loved one.

A season is not defined as much by an increment of time or the changing landscape as it is by a lesson learned or wisdom gained. And with each new season you will need a new set of skills and strengths. You will need endurance to face childbirth, and understanding to help you grieve a loss. Patience and determination will be essential as you climb the corporate ladder, and peace and joy will accompany you as you walk with your partner through all the fields of life.

The *Seasons of Life Meditations* were created to be a friend traveling with you as you experience the joys and sorrows of each season. They will console, energize, counsel, chide, and inspire. These meditations contain the gentle wisdom of those who have experienced many seasons of

. . . .

their own. While they may not completely understand your situation, the authors have been somewhere similar and can offer advice to help you understand yourself, your emotions, God, and your world.

The authors and editors wish you peace, wisdom, and love as you face all of your *Seasons of Life*.

In the other gardens
And all up the vale,
From the autumn bonfires
See the smoke trail!

Pleasant summer over
And all the summer flowers,
The red fire blazes,
The gray smoke towers.

Sing a song of seasons!
Something bright in all!
Flowers in the summer,
Fires in the fall!
—Robert Louis Stevenson,
Autumn Fires

*T*grew up in a small town in the southwest that held a fiesta each September. A ceremony to "burn away" troubles kicked off the festivities. On Friday night, thousands of cars joined together on the high school football field to watch the burning of Zozobra—Old Man Gloom.

Zozobra was a huge cloth and paper dummy with a frightening papier-maché head. His burning signified the end to all sadness for the fiesta period. I remember sitting on my family's car, watching Zozobra move his horrible head and long skeletal arms. At his feet, a fire-dancer jumped and leapt, waving two flaming sticks.

The dancer ignited Old Man Gloom at the climax of the dance. Huge crimson flames shot into the air as Zozobra burned.

In a matter of minutes, blackened wire and glowing scraps were all that remained. Old Man Gloom was gone for another year; we could all be happy.

Friends of mine now practice a similar rite during autumn with a bonfire party. They ask their guests to bring whatever they wish to get rid of. Tax returns, bills, and leftover scraps from home remodeling projects are among the items flung into the flames.

Autumn is the perfect time of year to "burn away" our worries and problems from the past and start with a clean slate.

Today, I will leave my troubles and hardships behind where they belong, in the past.

Without dark, there is light.
Without light, there is dark.

Fall brings cold, crisp mornings followed by warm, almost hot, days; black nights and bright days. Thus, it is a season of contrasts.

Contrast is necessary in our physical world because it's the only way we can perceive differences. An artist knows the benefit of black and white placed side by side on the canvas—the contrast makes the image more powerful.

Wouldn't it be wonderful if we could also tell differences so plainly in our own lives? We would know when we were in dark or light. It's possible.

There was a time, not too long ago, when I was trapped in the "gray"—the in-between. My life was "dullsville." Everything felt cloudy. I even went skiing (a favorite recreation) with close friends, but I didn't have a good time. The light had truly gone out of my life.

Luckily for me, a friend noticed something was amiss. She mentioned it to me. I shrugged my shoulders and said, "I dunno, I just feel off-base."

"So what are you doing about it?" she asked.

"Nothing," I said (which was the tact I was

using for most everything during this time). "I'm hoping it'll go away on its own."

But it didn't. Things got worse. I teetered on the brink of depression; I had fallen into the dark. It was then that I asked for help—from this friend and from God.

God brought back the light to my life. I re-learned a valuable lesson: I must first feel the light inside, through a close, personal relationship with God, before I can feel any light outside.

God, thank you for the light you bring to my life and thank you for the dark that is present so that I might know the difference between the two and know where I want to be.

Tis the last rose of summer
Left blooming alone;
All her lovely companions
Are faded and gone;
No flower of her kindred,
No rosebud is nigh,
To reflect back her blushes,
Or give sigh for sigh.
                                    —Thomas Moore

As the last blooms of summer fade away, frolicking children return to the classrooms leaving the neighborhoods silent and empty. No other event more exemplifies the contrasting nature of our feelings during autumn. On one hand we are happy to see our children go, ecstatic for the free time, but we are also saddened by their absence. This is particularly true when the last child starts school for the first time.

A close friend's youngest child starts kindergarten this fall, and she has mixed feelings. "I'm glad to finally have the free time to do things without being tied down," she says. "But I feel lonely, too, because he's my last child, my baby, and he's growing up."

We all experience good and bad feelings; it's part of human nature. But, society wants us to disregard or "get over" bad, negative feelings.

This is how our problems start—when we ignore our negative emotions.

The healthiest way to handle mixed emotions is to accept them. My friend plans to fill up her time with activities she's always wanted to do and to maximize the time she has with her child doing one-on-one activities. She also knows there may be rough times when she's depressed and lonely. These emotions are natural, a part of being human. It's what happens when things change.

Give me the strength to experience all of my emotions, positive as well as negative. Give me the foresight to learn from my feelings and to seek help when they become overwhelming.

> *And He said, "The kingdom of God is as if a man should scatter seed on the ground, and should sleep by night and rise by day, and the seed should sprout and grow, he himself does not know how. For the earth yields crops by itself: first the blade, then the head, after that the full grain in the head. But when the grain ripens, immediately he puts in the sickle, because the harvest has come."*
>
> *—Mark 4:26–29*

*L*abor and celebration are two traditional activities of the harvest season. First, the field workers toil to bring in the harvest when the fruit, vegetable, or grain has ripened. Then, everyone revels in the bounty of that harvest.

Ancient customs celebrating the harvest season have included parties, dances, fertility ceremonies, and feasts. Many of these practices have dwindled since the 19th century, but such cultures as the Pennsylvania Dutch and some Native Americans still repeat the sacred rites of harvest.

In nearly all religions and cultures a strong correlation exists between the earthly harvest and the spiritual one. The reaping of the soul is no less crucial than the reaping of the wheat. It also requires labor and celebration. For as a seed thrown on bare ground and denied food, water, or sunshine will perish, so will the seed of love, planted deep within our hearts at birth, perish without care and nurturing.

Today, I will nurture the seed of love in my heart, so that I, too, may share in the great harvest celebration of my soul.

November's sky is chill and drear,
November's leaf is red and sear.
—Sir Walter Scott, Marmion

*A*nyone who is familiar with colorizing—
the process of matching an individual's natural
coloring with a season of nature—knows that
fall is representative of warm colors. Red, orange, yellow, and brown are predominant fall
colors. They are called "warm" because of the
emotions one feels when around these colors.

Red represents passionate feelings, including
love, anger, and danger. Orange emanates
warmth and energy. And yellow gives off sunny,
bright messages. All of these colors communicate
with the subconscious, intuitive mind.

During the fall, colors send subconscious messages that make us feel loving, warm, and alive.
We find harmony with ourselves and the world if
we are attuned to the messages sent by the colors
of the season.

*Today, I will notice the colors that
nature displays at this time of the
year, and I will enjoy the effect they
have on me.*

A flower can bloom only if it's been nurtured along the way.

$\mathcal{A}$ colleague of mine is an avid gardener. She works her flower beds, meticulously digging up her dahlia bulbs and planting tulip and daffodil bulbs for the spring. The bulbs she plants in the fall are fertilized, the soil loosened and reworked. Dahlia bulbs require extra care to ensure they won't perish over the winter. They are dug up, hosed off, and packed away in sawdust for the winter, safe from freezing temperatures and rodents' sharp teeth.

This woman nurtures her bulbs with special care, for without it they won't bloom next spring. She's also an expert at nurturing her family. She ensures they have a clean home, good food, clothes to wear, and lots of fun activities. But this woman has no time left over to nurture herself. Without this nurturing, her personal blooms will soon wilt and die.

It's a sad fact that many of us treat ourselves much worse than we treat others. This is particularly true for women because the nurturing image has been instilled in us since birth. Self-nurturing is crucial, for only by nurturing ourselves can we even begin to nurture others. Find something to do today for yourself—take a walk alone, enjoy a long bath, read a good book. Look in the mirror and tell your reflection how proud you are of yourself and how much you love yourself.

Today, I will find the time to take care of my own needs.

> *Like the cold of snow in time of*
> *harvest*
> *Is a faithful messenger to those who*
> *send him,*
> *For he refreshes the soul of his*
> *masters.*
>
> —*Proverbs 25:13*

I met my neighbor at the park late one fall afternoon. He seemed so jubilant that I had to ask why.

"What a day!" he said. "My assistant called in sick. The boss reprimanded me for an unhappy client. Traffic was backed up all the way home."

"And you can smile?" I asked.

He grimaced. "Well, when I got home, I kissed my two children and wife hello, but my thoughts were still on the horrible day at the office. Luckily, my wife immediately noticed something was wrong. 'Take a walk,' she said. 'You look like you need a break. I'll explain it to the the kids.' So I did, and that's why I'm smiling. I feel a thousand times better now."

Perhaps some of us can relate to this man's experience. But how many of us have had this outcome? The more common scenario is to arrive home after a rough day and spend the rest of the evening in a daze, mulling over the day's unhappy events.

We should all be so fortunate to have a perceptive partner, as this man does. She was the fresh air he needed that day. He desperately required that time alone to clear his mind of his troubles.

When we are lucky enough to have someone who seems connected and empathetic to our feelings and needs, the effect is much like the refreshing, invigorating first frost of autumn. And the message seems just as clear as if it came from God himself.

Give me the clarity to be sensitive to another's needs and feelings today.

> *Boys and girls come out to play,*
> *The moon doth shine as bright as*
> *day.*
> —*18th Century Nursery Rhyme*

The full moon closest to the first day of fall is dubbed the harvest moon. The harvest moon gets its name because of the additional light it gives farmers trying to win the race against the first frost. And, for reasons known mainly to astronomers, it is larger and brighter than most other full moons.

There's a different feel to the moon during the fall. The harvest moon is revered, even welcomed, for the extra light it gives when daylight is dwindling, and for the significance it carries for a bountiful harvest and future.

If I'm fortunate enough to see the harvest moon, I'll bundle up and take a walk. I am always awed by the moonlit landscape and the moonshadows. The air feels refreshing and invigorating—almost magical. This experience, when shared with a friend or a child, is very special.

When I see the harvest moon this fall, I will imagine it is a sign of good things to come.

Give us this day our daily bread.
—Matthew 6:11

I can't think of anything more comforting than the smell of baked bread. In fact, realtors suggest that clients bake a loaf to create a homey atmosphere while their house is being shown.

Bread baking is an art, and can be therapeutic as well. Kneading the dough is similar to throwing a pot on a potter's wheel—it makes one more aware of one's inner self or center. Just as clay has to be kept in the center of the wheel so the pot will be symmetrical, we, too, have to be centered in our own lives to keep from becoming off-balance.

Most days I feel about as centered as a skater on the end of a "crack-the-whip" line. I'm tugged from all angles—by the needs of my children, the wants of my husband, the desires of the PTA or the Scouts or the school, and the demands of my career. Sometimes I'm jerked around so much that I feel I'll crash into a wall.

I crave activities that help me get back to my center when my life gets this harried. One of those activities is making bread (not with the new bread machines, though—the old way, by hand). I love to grab a spongy handful of dough and push and pound out my frustrations. Eventually, the repetitive kneading slows the constant parade of thoughts through my mind and brings me back to my center.

I will do some activity today that makes me feel more centered and balanced.

How far that little candle throws his beams!
So shines a good deed in a naughty world.
—Shakespeare, The Merchant of Venice

*D*uring autumn, days grow shorter and nights grow longer. I'm particularly sensitive to the lack of natural light, so the increasing darkness that comes with fall depresses me.

While today we can quickly shut out the dark with a simple flip of the switch, we forget that a nearly perfect, low-cost source of light comes from a candle. A few photographers even choose candlelight over harsh incandescent or fluorescent lighting because it's softer and more becoming to their subjects. Legend purports that Abraham Lincoln did his schoolwork by candlelight.

A candle is a symbol of reverence and ritual. Some groups, such as Girl Scouts U.S.A., incorporate candlelighting into their ceremonies. A lit candle represents spiritual illumination and consciousness. Even today, many people meditate by candlelight. One need only to stare at the wavering flame to see how mesmerizing it can be.

Candlelight draws us back in time to a source

of light used for thousands of autumns. As night cloaks the world in darkness and the fall wind whips up the leaves, I love to plan a candlelight dinner. My family thinks it's great and we save energy, too. Sometimes, we even pretend we're living in a time when candles were the only source of light.

Tonight, I will have a candlelight dinner to brighten up a dark autumn night.

When it's dark outside, I can feel the sunshine inside.

A telltale sign of autumn in the southwestern United States is strings of red chilies, called "ristras," hanging in front of white stucco homes. The chilies ripen into a deep red color in late fall, are picked, and then hand-strung. Outside, they dry and are preserved for the winter as seasonings for the spicy dishes of this part of the world.

An ancient Native American legend tells how the coyote grumbled to the Goddess of Seasons about the cold and dark winter. Seeing his point, she instructed him to grind chilies into a fine powder. He tasted the powder, and immediately felt the warmth of the sun on his tongue. He no longer felt cold. Later, people learned to make ristras for the same purpose.

I love to cook Mexican food when it's dark and dreary outside. As I taste the hot, spicy flavors, I recall the legend, and I remember sunny days at the beach, walks in the desert, and the feel of the hot summer sun on my face.

Lord, thank you for the things that bring memories of sunnier days.

> *. . . To set budding more,*
> *And still more, later flowers for the*
> *bees,*
> *Until they think warm days will*
> *never cease,*
> *For Summer has o'er-brimm'd their*
> *clammy cells.*
> —*John Keats,* To Autumn

I enrolled in field botany one fall quarter in college. Anyone who has taken a class similar to this knows one of the requisites is a field collection of flowers. *Great,* I thought. *Instead of writing a term paper, I get credit for picking flowers.*

Needless to say, I worked harder on that field collection than any other class that fall. Nearly every flower I found was of the immense and diverse family of sunflowers or asters. There are hundreds of species of asters. To make matters even worse, each flower head is made up of hundreds of tiny, individual flowers. And, it's those minuscule individual flowers that have to be dissected and recorded.

Sunflower heads are usually crawling with bees and other insects, ensuring more sunflowers to color our world and honey to enjoy. Roadsides are lined with asters and sunflowers during the fall. This fall, take a moment to really look at a sunflower; touch its center (watch out for the bees!); see if you can discern all the tiny flowers. It's fascinating how something so simple-looking to the naked eye can actually be so complex— another of God's incredibly intricate creations.

Thank you, God, for the beauty you bring to the earth during autumn.

> *And let us not grow weary while*
> *doing good, for in due season we*
> *shall reap if we do not lose heart.*
> —*Galatians 6:9*

*R*ecently I had one of those nights we all like to forget. Dirty clothes littered the hallway. Screaming and yelling reverberated off the walls. *What's wrong with this picture?* I asked myself. *Here I am with the laundry and the kids while my husband's wining and dining out of town on a business trip.*

I sighed and walked through the bathroom doorway to referee another fight. An hour later, after lots of cajoling, I had the kids seated on the couch and ready for a bedtime story. I glanced at the clock—only thirty minutes until bedtime and, finally, some peace and quiet.

"Mommy," my youngest daughter said.

"What?" I asked.

"I love you."

My other daughter chimed in. "I love you, too, Mommy," she said.

My eyes filled with tears. I hugged both girls and murmured, "I love you." Then I said a silent prayer.

I'm sure every parent or caregiver experiences these feelings over and over. The childcare tasks seem endless and thankless, until that one moment when we catch a glimpse of the fruits of our labor.

There is no career more important than that of raising our young. It's also the most difficult. The innocent little ones can try our patience to the extreme. Instead of reducing the labor, they increase the work exponentially.

No one ever said it would be easy on this earth. And if it were, if there were no challenges, what would drive us, make us learn, and help us grow?

Along with the spiritual harvest of our souls is the work that gets us to that point. Possibly, it is the hardest work we will ever do; the most difficult to stick with. God promises: If we persevere, we will be rewarded. He shows us this in small ways (if we will notice) as he did for me on that night not too long ago.

I will look for God's handiwork in even the most menial task today, and be grateful for this life he has given me and for loved ones he has surrounded me with.

> *If you grieve for the dead, morn also for those who are born into the world; for as the one thing is of nature, so is the other too of nature.*
> —St. John Chrysostom

Fall is a time of endings and beginnings. In the span of two months, a close friend of mine came face to face with birth as well as with death. One warm, sunny day in late September, her only daughter went into labor with her first child. Twenty hours later, my friend had a crinkly, red, newborn granddaughter.

The birth of any child is a miracle to behold, but there are few things more wonderful than the birth of a grandchild. My friend was ecstatic with this birth. There seemed to be new vitality to her outlook. Until she received the phone call in November.

Her mother died in her sleep. In a matter of hours, my friend's vitality dropped as she boarded a plane bound for California and the ensuing funeral.

Instead of joy and celebration, this woman felt emptiness and fear. She had lost the one person who brought her into this world. There was no longer the option to go home to Mom if her life's plans didn't work out.

My friend had much to resolve through the grieving process. But she also had much to be thankful for: a new granddaughter and memories from a lifetime of love from her mother.

Sages tell us that life and death are so closely related that we never understand until we pass over the line. God further instructs us that we have the opportunity to be connected to the afterlife through meditation and prayer.

The same joyous place that springs us into life at our birth calls us back upon our death. Thank you, Lord, for the opportunity you have given me to experience this joyous place while I am mortal.

The harvest of our creativity can come only when the mind is quiet.

*D*on't you hate it when you really need to think clearly and your mind is muddled with all types of thought-clutter? It's sort of like a computer screaming an "insufficient disk space" error message. *Bleep*, we go on overload because of too much stuff crowding our brain waves. That's when it's time to take a break.

Brenda Ueland[1] recommended we all find idle time in each day. Rather than being non-productive, such time is actually the only way creativity will find an outlet. "So you see the imagination needs molding—long, inefficient happy idling, dawdling and puttering," she says.

An artist needs such contemplation to see a vision; a writer, a storyline; and all of us, solutions to our problems. It's also the only way intuition can be heard, what some call communication from the unconscious mind.

If I can relax and calm my mind, I start to see solutions to some of my problems. When I dream, for instance, I get an idea that I would never have thought about during my waking hours.

Looking for ways to make idle time will help in calming our minds. Hobbies, such as cross-stitching, quilting, knitting, gardening, or wood-carving occupies our hands and slows down our thoughts. A famous mystery writer plays solitaire to help him plot and plan his books. I like to take a long walk each day. For me, it's a brief solace from my hectic day.

Today, I will find some time to be idle, to quiet my fast-paced life.

For so the LORD said to me, "I will take My rest, and I will look from My dwelling place like clear heat in sunshine, like a cloud of dew in the heat of harvest."

—Isaiah 18:4

*N*othing is more noticeable than fresh dew on a fall morning. It is a refreshing contrast to the dry, hot days of the harvest season. So distinct, in fact, that if it happens in the middle of the day, one couldn't miss it.

God's direction is much like that. If we are tuned in, we can actually see and hear his message very clearly, very distinctly. It's sort of like thinking of one's self as a radio receiver. The key is to tune in to God's frequency.

I know a couple who had a certain amount of money budgeted to purchase their first home. A real estate agent showed them a cute bungalow which had been on the market for some time. They each felt, intuitively, this was the one.

The husband felt he had a divine message from God directing him to offer a certain amount of money; no less, no more. So they phoned their agent with the offer. The agent was reluctant to forward the offer to the seller, but she did anyway.

. . . .

Two hours later she phoned them back. "This sounds ludicrous, but the seller countered for $2,000 more than you offered. It's a great deal for that house."

The wife wanted to accept the contract, but her husband said, "No, I believe the Lord wanted me to pay this amount and that's our final offer."

The agent tried to persuade him otherwise, but he wouldn't waver. One week later, the agent contacted the couple in person—the seller had accepted their offer!

God's direction is certainly not that clear in my life. But if it were, I know things would go a lot smoother.

God, give me the capability to hear your message as clearly as possible in my everyday life.

. . . .

It's easier to focus on the one brown patch rather than the expanse of green lawn surrounding it.

I talked with a friend the other day. She told me that she and her husband just paid off their mortgage. I was amazed. Now that was an accomplishment!

"How did you celebrate?" I asked her.

"What do you mean?" she responded.

"Didn't you make a big deal out of it?"

"Not really. It was just another day."

We, as a society, don't celebrate enough. We certainly do enough complaining, though. You only have to watch the evening news or read the daily paper to see where our emphasis lies: on the pain, the negative, and the suffering.

It's important for us to look for small things, small accomplishments to celebrate. And if we can't find any of those, we can make some up. Some parenting books even recommend each person have one day (a week or month) designated as his or her special day. That person gets to choose what's for dinner and receives special treatment the entire day. You could even make a banner or have the person wear a crown. "Queen" or "King for a Day." Sounds hokey, but the person wearing the crown feels pretty good, especially if it's a young child.

It's a good idea to make a big deal of any small thing: getting the dog's shots, a good school paper, a clean house, or paying off a credit card.

I will find some small thing to celebrate today and make it a big thing.

You crown the year with Your
goodness,
And Your paths drip with
abundance.
They drop on the pastures of the
wilderness,
And the little hills rejoice on every
side.
The pastures are clothed with flocks;
The valleys also are covered with
grain;
They shout for joy, they also sing.
—Psalm 65:11–13

*A*utumn, for my grandmother, was the busiest time of year. She picked the fruit from the trees, harvested the vegetables, and spent hours in her kitchen over a steaming caldron, canning and preserving. The results of the harvest were on visual display in the rows and rows of canned green beans, tomatoes, peaches, jams, and jellies in her pantry.

I still do some canning and freezing in the fall, but the results of my labor over the past year are not on visual display like those jars in my grandmother's pantry. Anything that isn't visible isn't tangible. If I can't see the results, how can I be grateful? Did I accomplish anything this past year?

By the very act of living, I have made some mark on the earth, even if small—perhaps through my children, my husband, my friends, my occupation, or my church. Whatever the activity, there has been some accomplishment made this past year.

Take a piece of paper and write down all the wonderful things that happened to you over the past year. They don't have to be earth-shattering, either. In fact, it's the little accomplishments that really mean the most and for which we need to be proud.

I did this exercise because I found it hard to come up with any tangible accomplishments for our family. It was a very hard year for me and I was reluctant to revisit it. My oldest daughter had problems in school, my husband struggled with clinical depression, and I had an exhausting summer taking on the physical and emotional support of the family.

But as I forced myself to think of the year's high points, the accomplishments started to come to mind. Small, subtle things, like how my daughter got back on track and my husband and I entered counseling and my acceptance of our living situation, were actually major accomplishments. After doing this exercise, I saw how God had been working in my life over the past year. It humbled me that I hadn't noticed his work before.

I will be proud of all my accomplishments (minor and major) this past year, and grateful to God. If I can't think of any accomplishments, I will be grateful for simply making it through another year.

*Offer to God thanksgiving,
And pay your vows to the Most
High.*

—Psalm 50:14

In the United States and Canada we have a holiday set aside for the purpose of saying thanks for the year's fruitful harvest—Thanksgiving.

How much thanksgiving do you practice at other times of the year? If you're like me, very little, except, perhaps, at meals. (My children even fight over whose turn it is to say grace—a bone of contention that we are working on!)

Food is not the only thing to be thankful for, although it is an important gift. Our families, friends, homes, and material possessions are all blessings, too. And, most important, the fact that we wake up and can take another breath of life is reason enough to give thanks. Without this breath we wouldn't be alive and be able to enjoy the other things around us.

Do I really appreciate my life? Sometimes I look at my life as a burden—something I have to endure. This particularly seems the case when I'm experiencing powerful emotions or when I'm under stress, like the time I was late for an appointment, the phone kept ringing, and just as I got the kids out the door the dog soiled the rug. When things are bad it's hard for me to be grateful. My typical response is to wish things were different.

A little gratitude goes a long way. If I just close my eyes and say, "Thank you, Lord, for this life you have given me," I immediately feel better. And I think he does too.

I will give thanks for my blessings each and every day.

The gift of life unwraps itself through time; all we need to do is sit back and enjoy its contents.

watched my daughter unwrap a birthday gift addressed to her from her grandparents. She couldn't wait to open it and see what was inside. We are all enthralled with a present addressed to us. Most of the time, we don't care what's inside. The fun is the surprise element. But, if we have an expectation about what kind of gift we want, we're frequently disappointed by the contents. And we sometimes exchange it.

The gift of life is similar. It constantly unwraps itself and we experience what's inside. When we have expectations about our lives, we are usually disappointed by the way things turn out. When we're open to whatever happens, we are rewarded.

Lord, help me surrender and let my life unfold without expectation so I can enjoy your gift of life more fully.

> *Change and decay in all around I*
> *see;*
> *O thou, who changest not, abide*
> *with me.*
>
> —*Henry Francis Lyte,*
> Abide with Me

I was hiking with my family one warm fall afternoon in the alpine meadows beneath Mount Rainier. The blueberries were ripe; the leaves bright red and orange. And there was a strange smell in the air.

"What's that odor?" a passerby asked me on the trail.

"It's the decaying vegetation," I answered.

He held his nose and walked on. Sure enough, most of the flowers, grasses, and shrubs were in the process of dropping leaves and dying back for the winter. Dead and decaying vegetative matter lay everywhere and a very pungent odor hung in the air. Unlike the gentleman who questioned me, I didn't find the smell distasteful.

Change and decay are facts of life in our world. We see them, smell them, feel them, and sometimes hear them, especially when the physical world changes around us as it does with the seasons. Nature depends on decay to survive. Without dying leaves, new leaves cannot come out in the spring. From decay springs change. And nature is based upon change.

Change can be disconcerting in our lives. A change of living area, change in family (by adding or subtracting a member), and a change of job all constitute life stressors. Too many changes can be disastrous, as my family found out firsthand. In the span of a few months we moved, changed jobs, and had a baby!

If the outside changes get too chaotic, I can always be with God inside my heart. It's the only place that never changes.

Only through change can I achieve my full potential.

*F*all signifies a period of physical change for the world between the flourishing period of summer and the languishing period of winter. Even though fall and winter are not normally thought of as times of growth, change by its very nature signifies growth. For example, without change a natural lake becomes eutrophic. A new source of water must enter and leave the lake to keep it from becoming stagnant.

The same principle applies to the world. What would happen if we were immersed in a constant season without change? In C. S. Lewis' *The Lion, the Witch and the Wardrobe*², the fantasy world of Narnia was imprisoned by the White Witch in constant winter (a winter without Christmas to boot). The balance was upset and Narnia was in trouble.

Our lives can be like this sometimes. We avoid change because it brings risks of the unknown, which we fear. If we move to this place, what will happen? If we accept this promotion, will we be able to perform?

Change is stressful, no doubt about it. Too much change can be detrimental. Too little change can also be detrimental. Some change is good.

Lord, let me embrace the changes that occur in my life as a necessary component to my growth and development.

He shall be like a tree
  Planted by the rivers of water,
That brings forth its fruit in its
      season,
  Whose leaf also shall not wither;
And whatever he does shall prosper.
            —Psalm 1:3

There are few things more delicious than the crisp sweet taste of a just-picked apple. I can remember going to the orchards as a child during the fall, after a long dusty ride over bumpy roads. Towering ladders leaned against trees laden with ripe apples. There were apples as yellow as tennis balls and as red as ripe tomatoes. We were given buckets and sent among the trees to pick as many as we could carry.

The good ones were always out of our reach. To the chagrin of my brothers, Mom wouldn't let us climb to the very top of the ladders. That was reserved for Dad. He always got the sweetest apples from the top.

Some we took home to eat, but we made cider in the creaking, wooden press with others. Dad would grind away on the handle as we threw in apple after apple. Chunks and stems flew everywhere. A worker helped us load the mash into the press, which would take three or four of us to crank.

The result was the finest cider we had ever tasted. We drank right out of the jug. Sometimes we would gulp down a whole gallon before we even got to the car. The cider we pressed ourselves always tasted better than the cider we bought from the orchard owners.

Sometimes I compare my life to those apples and the pressed cider from my childhood. When I strive and work hard, the rewards are plentiful and sweet. When I live my life actively, participating in decisions and actions, I feel better about myself, as if I'm a partner in my own destiny.

Today, I will approach my life actively, and make things happen. I will enjoy the results that come from my labor and efforts.

Who I am on the outside has nothing to do with who I am on the inside; who I am on the inside has everything to do with who I am on the outside.

When my friend's youngest child started kindergarten in the fall, she was left with an empty house and lots of time on her hands. For the first month she kept busy cleaning closets she never got to, filtering through old summer clothes, and fishing out winter garments. She even started to paint the interior of her home. And she was always there for the kids when they got home—a rarity in her neighborhood because most other women worked outside the home.

In mid-October my friend ran out of jobs to do, as well as the desire to do the jobs. She found herself drawn more and more to daytime television. Sometimes she wouldn't even get dressed until noon.

Her husband suggested she volunteer at the school, but that wasn't the answer. Something was missing from her life; something was wrong and she didn't know what it was. One morning my friend woke up and looked at herself in the bathroom mirror. "Who is this person?" she asked.

If we bank our identity on others or on our accomplishments (such as our career), we risk the loss of this identity when these things change or go away. And change they will!

God made us perfect in his image. We are entirely worthy in his eyes. All the other things we do while on this earth are merely what we do, not who we are. Our identity is who we are inside, not on the surface. We are children of God and, as such, worthwhile and loving persons.

My self-worth does not depend upon anything I do while in this world. Instead, my self-worth is firmly based upon God's unconditional acceptance and love.

*Miracles occur when something is
taken from its raw form and refined
into something even better.*

Cranberries are among many berries that
ripen in the fall. I used to forage for cranberries
along the shores of Lake Superior, collecting
them from the small bushes that grew in the
boggy cracks between the shoreline rocks.

Raw cranberries don't taste very good.
They're mealy and sour. But baked in breads or
muffins or cooked with sweeteners, cranberries
have a unique flavor that many people enjoy.

This is an example of how a raw ingredient is
improved with the processing done after it's harvested. A friend of mine feels the same way about
himself.

"I look at myself as a lump of clay. Under
God's guidance, I'm smoothed and shaped over
time," he says. The challenge for us, this friend
feels, is to remain flexible enough so that God
can shape us.

It's not an easy challenge. I always know how
I want my life to run; I must feel as mealy as a
raw cranberry in God's hands. I wonder if he
works harder on me or if he waits until I've softened, when I've given up or become vulnerable. I
think it's the latter. Thus, it is to my benefit to be

. . . .

as flexible as possible, amenable to God's work in my life.

Lord, help me to remain open to your handiwork so that your divine hands can do miracles.

. . . .

*A child learns more by observing
than by listening.*

Autumn is usually the time of year when schools schedule open houses and parent-teacher conferences. My husband and I got a real jolt at our daughter's conference. Even though we constantly tell her about the value of school, she seems not to hear us. It's as if what we say goes in one ear and out the other. At one point, we even had her hearing checked.

Teachers and counselors agree that a child learns most effectively by example or doing. Lectures are the least productive means to teach anyone. The messages are always more effective if they're conveyed by actions.

That's been God's message to us from the beginning: Let your actions speak, not your words. This is why people readily condemn ministers and priests whose behavior is contrary to what they've preached. Hypocrites are not tolerated.

There are few of us who are not, in some way, hypocritical. I find myself lecturing my daughter to get her homework and chores done early, but this year I procrastinated filing my tax return and did it the night before it was due. When my daughter yells at me or her younger sister, I scream back, telling her not to yell. If I'm conscious of my actions, I'll stop myself and ask, *Is this the message I want to send to my children?*

Today I will be conscious of my actions. I know they will be more powerful than anything I might say.

Let your light so shine before men,
that they may see your good works
and glorify your Father in heaven.
—*Matthew 5:16*

A wise teacher once told me about his "light bulb theory." He said, "A light bulb does not have the words 'light bulb' written all over it. If it did, no light could shine through all the letters. Instead, the light bulb just is. Its nature is to shine."

Have you ever noticed how moths, flies, and every other flying insect seem to flock to light bulbs? The saying "a moth to the flame" comes from this phenomenon. The same attraction exists for us human beings.

I've noticed I like to be around people who seem high on life and give off a type of light through their love. It feels good to be in their presence. Yet, these people don't lecture me or ask me to believe in their concepts or ideas. They just emit positive energy by their actions and behaviors.

Today, I will let my own light bulb shine.

*If you eat a toadstool and don't die,
it's a mushroom.*

—*Anonymous*

Where I live, fall is known as mushroom season. Mushroom buyers flock to the backroads and sit in their trucks and vans, paying top dollar for gourmet wild mushrooms. If one knows one's mushrooms, one can make a bundle.

I have a friend who is a mushroom picker. I've gone picking with her on a few occasions, and it's amazing how similar all the varieties look to my untrained eye.

"This one is really poisonous," she says, pointing to a nondescript brown mushroom. "But this one is delicious." And she digs up one similar to the first.

The key to mushroom picking is knowing the differences between the poisonous and the edible varieties. For instance, sorrels have a solid, ridged undersurface rather than the fleshy folds of most other mushrooms. But that's not the only characteristic. A mushroom picker has to be an expert. To be otherwise is to toy with death.

Picking and choosing what the world offers isn't as graphic as a wrong mushroom choice, but it can sometimes be just as deadly. One only has to watch the evening news or read a newspaper to see how other human beings have gone wrong. Unfortunately, we're supposed to learn from others' mistakes, but that isn't easy. A better way to learn would be to have a diagnostic tool, much like a "mushroom key," that would point the way towards the right, healthy choices we must make. The Bible can be that key.

I will meditate on God's word and direction today as a key to help me make the right choices in my life.

*Strange to see how a good dinner
and feasting reconciles everybody.*
—Samuel Pepys, Diary

*H*uge feasts that celebrate the bountiful harvests have always been a ritual of the autumn season. Our Thanksgiving holiday finds its roots in this tradition.

In the Hawaiian culture, feasting is considered an opportunity to be close to God. The Hawaiians believe that food is a gift and, as such, should be appreciated with special reverence. A Hawaiian feast is an act of communion with God.

With shorter days and longer nights at this time of the year comes the opportunity for dining together with friends. And, whenever two human beings are communicating, God has found an avenue for his message.

At this time of year, I like to invite friends over for an impromptu dinner. If we are grateful for the blessings we received over the past year, the meal becomes fulfilling spiritually as well as physically.

*I will make an opportunity for
fellowship by breaking bread with
others today.*

I have to be careful what I ask for because I might get it.

*H*ave you ever wanted something and then received it, although probably not in the way you expected? This happens frequently to me and it's unnerving.

In my business, peaks and valleys are the name of the game; feast or famine. I finished an intense project under a very tight deadline and looked forward to a time when my life wouldn't be so hectic.

After I met my deadline, I spent the next two weeks recovering, in a daze. It was as if I weren't inspired to write. (I've since talked with other writers and they tell me the same thing happens to them.)

I found myself secretly wishing for another project, something to motivate me. In a matter of weeks, my wishes came true. Whether I was ready or not, I was back against tight deadlines and lots of work.

Now that I look back on it, I realize God answered my request. I truly believe, with trust and patience, God answers our prayers in ways that are even better than we first imagine. I wonder if there's a part of us that instinctively knows what we need, when we need it, and how to obtain it (with God's help).

God is waiting to give us what we need. All we have to do is ask.

*Trust in the LORD with all your
heart,
And lean not on your own
understanding;
In all your ways acknowledge Him,
And He shall direct your paths.*
　　　　　　　　—*Proverbs 3:5, 6*

A man I know had a hard time adjusting to life after his divorce. He lived alone in an apartment. Nights and weekends were the most difficult. In the beginning he watched a lot of televised sporting events. When that got boring, he visited the neighborhood tavern, but soon grew tired of the smoky, depressing atmosphere.

Many times he cried himself to sleep. He said it never occurred to him to ask for help. For months he tried to tough it out and get through the pain.

One night, when things got really bad, he stared at the ceiling for a long time, feeling the hurt and loneliness inside. The familiar tears started to roll from the corners of his eyes.

A prayer he recalled from his childhood came to mind: "The LORD is my shepherd; I shall not want. . . ." (Psalm 23). He fell asleep mumbling the words to himself. It was the most comforting sleep he'd had in a long time.

Since then he has learned to ask for help. He regularly turns to God for help and guidance. And he also talks to others, such as those in the same predicament. While he doesn't feel he's recovered from the divorce, he knows he doesn't have to suffer alone.

Autumn is a time when many of us experience intense emotions. It's a time of change, and change affects our emotions. If I find myself suffering from sadness and depression and things get too negative for me to handle, I know I need to ask for help.

God stands ready to support us, to show us the way, and to hold our hands as we walk. The only catch is that we have to first ask for his help. God will help only those who solicit his guidance.

God cannot answer our cries for help unless we knock on his door. I will learn to ask for His help whenever I need it.

> *God's works are good. This truth to*
> *prove*
> *Around the world I need not move;*
> *I do it by the nearest pumpkin.*
> —*Jean de la Fontaine*

A pile of orange pumpkins in front of a fruit stand or grocery store is a symbol of fall. Roaming through a pumpkin patch to pick out that perfect specimen for a jack-o-lantern or pie is an activity enjoyed by thousands during the month of October.

God is omniscient, omnipresent, and omnipotent. Every object or living creature has the mark of God's hands on it. Everything was created by God and everything is connected by this common thread.

Sometimes we think of God's work only in majestic proportions—a mountain range or a cathedral or witnessing the miraculous recovery of a terminally ill patient. But evidence of God's presence can also be seen in a droplet of rain, a single snowflake, the first smile on a baby's face, and a small green shoot coming up through the snow.

Life vibrates in everything we hear, see, and smell in the world around us. God is everywhere—from the sun to the tiniest grain of sand.

This is the miracle of creation for which we need to be grateful.

I will notice God's presence in everything I experience today.

*Finally, brethren, whatever things
are true, whatever things are noble,
whatever things are just, whatever
things are pure, whatever things are
lovely, whatever things are
of good report, if there be any
virtue and if there is anything
praiseworthy—meditate on these
things.*

—*Philippians 4:8*

*H*ave you ever noticed how good you feel
when you're around people who seem enthused
with life? I do. I don't think it's coincidence either. I believe God planned the world in such a
way that we would feel good when around the
beautiful, the pure, and the just. In fact, prophets
tell us to look at our souls as if God programmed
two very opposing feelings within every human
being.

The first is called a "cup of joy." Whenever we
drink from this cup we feel great, incredible, and
happy. Things that surround us, such as our
loved ones, the beauty of nature, and the miracle
of creation, make us drink from this cup.

But God also gave us a "cup of sorrow." And
He did so because this was the only way we
could tell what the cup of joy tasted like. He ar-

ranged for the cup of joy to taste imminently better than the cup of sorrow, but we would never know that until we tasted the cup of sorrow.

Unfortunately, we have one problem: The human race has become hooked on the cup of sorrow. In fact, we're so preoccupied with how bad it tastes that it seems we have completely forgotten about the cup of joy.

Meditating on the good in the world, on the beautiful, the joyful, and the happy, will help us to rediscover our own cups of joy. If we redirect our focus to these things and contemplate them, we will be drinking from the cup of joy and be reminded how wonderful it is to be alive.

God, help me to find the "cup of joy" within myself and to drink freely of its nectar.

> *Laugh, and the world laughs with*
> *   you;*
> *   Weep, and you weep alone,*
> *For the sad old earth must borrow*
> *   its mirth,*
> *   But has trouble enough of its*
> *   own.*
> —*Ella Wheeler Wilcox*, Solitude

There's not enough humor in the world. When some of my friends start getting the autumn blues they play "Mad Dog," the game written about by Laura Ingalls Wilder.[3] First they turn off all the lights in the house and someone hides. The rest of the family look for that person. When they get close, the hidden person jumps out and screams. They end up running and laughing throughout the house. If tension is in the air and they find themselves at each other's throats, one of them says, "Let's play Mad Dog," and it always makes them laugh and feel better.

Laughter is one of the best ways to cope with and beat the effects of a stressful life. No matter how much pain or suffering we see, if there is a smile, a giggle, or a laugh, we know things are okay.

Laughter is contagious! It's the best thing we can give back to the world. And it's the finest medicine for ourselves. I find that if I look at some old photos or a school album, there's always something that makes me laugh. Think of something funny that happened to you once. Call up a friend. Better yet, rent or go to a funny movie, watch a comedy show on television, or play a humorous game with your family.

Today, I will find something to laugh about and share it with someone who is special to me.

*No Spring, nor Summer beauty
hath such grace,
As I have seen in one Autumnal
face.*
—*John Donne,* The Autumnal

I grew up near my grandmother and my great-aunt. One was a widow, the other a spinster. As a child, I resented the time my mother made me spend with these two elderly ladies. It felt so stifling to be in their house when I longed to be outside in the fresh air with kids my own age. I'd fidget about until I could finally escape.

Now that I'm older and both my grandmother and great-aunt have long since died, I remember conversations with them far more vividly than my playtimes outside. I recall one instance in particular when my great-aunt told me about growing up in Germany. I watched her eyes light up and thought I saw a glow around her white hair. She looked beautiful.

Unlike other cultures, we have lost the valuable resource of our older society. We put them out of the way in nicely-packaged senior centers and nursing homes. Although these establishments provide the type of care which usually cannot be given elsewhere, by doing so we've lost a vast source of wisdom and experience. No wonder our children fear the aged—they are kept away from them. Many children, like my own, see their grandparents only a few days out of the year, if at all.

There are winds of hope, though. Some schools and daycare centers have tapped the senior population for help. It's great for those seniors who are interested, and even greater for the children.

Now is a prime opportunity to spend time with those in their autumn of life, to be in the presence of the grace that comes only after a lifetime of trials and joys.

Today I will seek out someone who is years ahead of me in life, either in person or by phone.

> *Praise the ripe field, not the green corn.*
>
> —*Irish proverb*

*F*or most of my life I lived in the southwestern part of the United States. I always marvel at how cornfields seem to thrive in spite of the extreme climatic conditions of this region—long periods of scorching heat, cracked soils, and torrential rains.

Corn is sacred to Hopis, Navajos, and countless other societies, including the Mayan culture of Central and South America. It is considered a sustenance of body and soul and a necessary ingredient in ritual after ritual.

Corn, to a Hopi, is a reflection of the human life span. First, the seeds are planted in moist, tilled soil. The seed is nurtured, just as a Hopi child is nurtured. Everyone prays for the corn to grow, just as they pray for the children to grow.

With this careful attention the corn grows into green stalks reaching toward the immense blue sky. Under the blazing summer sun, the leaves wilt and close up, as a human does under the pressure of challenge. The rains come and, as if by magic, the corn rejuvenates, ready to reproduce. People do the same when showered with love and understanding.

. . . .

The culmination of the cycle comes when the corn is ready to be harvested. This is the fruit of the Hopis' labor and faith.

After the harvest, the old canes are pushed over and returned to the earth, as people are when their time is over. (In the Hopi language, the same word is used for spent corn and for a spent person.)

Each step in the process is crucial. Only through carelessness or lack of effort and spirit will the earth deny the Hopi its corn. The entire process requires intense faith and prayer to work. And as a result, the harvested corn is the mainstay of the Hopi society.

It would be wonderful to be as attuned to this seasonal cycle as the Hopi, living my life as a simple mirror of the life stages of a corn plant. Each step in the process from birth to death would be crucial, a building block for the next. Every stage would have an obvious purpose and I wouldn't feel so lost along the road of life. The tasks of childhood, adolescence, and adulthood would all lead to the ultimate harvest of my soul.

I know not when my own harvest will come, but I must prepare for it by tending my seed and nurturing my plant along the way.

. . . .

For the ignorant, old age is as winter; for the learned, it is a harvest.

—Jewish proverb

A close friend of mine recently retired from her job after nearly thirty years of service. Her office held a retirement luncheon in her honor and presented her with a commendation and several nice gifts. "It was a nice send-off," she said.

The woman had been an outstanding, intelligent, and productive employee. Yet, by her fifty-fifth birthday she was no longer of use. Of course, it was her decision to leave, but she experienced what many retirees do today when her employment ceased—a loss of self-worth.

Our society's population pyramid is top-heavy. Our largest segment, the baby boomers, is approaching retirement in the next few decades. Not only is this going to be a financial drain on the country's retirement system (already a concern to legislators), but an entire generation will leave the business world. And so will the corresponding knowledge and experience.

Some companies are progressive enough to realize the value of their older, more experienced employees and have assigned them the task of training new employees. Unfortunately, this is a rarity. More common is the practice of reducing senior employees' responsibilities and putting them "out to pasture" in a job where they simply wait for retirement. Company policy interprets these employees as having passed beyond their productive and useful years. The wise person knows otherwise.

I will look to someone more experienced than I for wisdom; the resulting knowledge I gain will be invaluable.

Two halves brought together in marriage do not make a whole.

I was married one day in October and my life was forever changed. Marriage means different things to different people. A pastor friend of mine summed it up for me by saying, "Marriage is a process whereby a man and a woman are both inspired to reach higher plateaus than if they were alone. It's instant defeat if one looks to the marriage partner for satisfaction. One must approach the altar a whole person and through the marriage process, two whole persons become more effective together than apart."

We can apply these same principles to our daily lives. Our biggest lesson may just be that our fulfillment doesn't come from any outside source, be it another person or material possessions. Rather, our gratification comes from inside our hearts and through a personal relationship with our creator. Thus satisfied, we are then equipped to give back to the rest of the world.

God, help me to become a complete and fulfilled person through your love and acceptance.

*T*have a friend who is an intelligent young woman. On the surface she has everything going for her—financial security and a rewarding career. Underneath, she's unhappy. She wants to marry and is on the lookout for the "right" guy. Other friends who know this woman are amazed no man has found her. They say, "She has everything going for her. Why hasn't she married?"

I'm sure there are other issues here, but I feel the reason this friend may not have found what she is looking for is because she's immersed in the search. I have another friend who wished she could find a husband. Interestingly enough, once she stopped wishing, she met the man she eventually married.

When we're not looking for something, we usually find it or, more accurately, it finds us. It works with objects as well. An instructor told me if you lose an object, you can use your intuition to find that object again by letting go of the search. (Of course, this is much more difficult if it's a set of car keys and I have to leave at a certain time. All the more reason I should keep an extra set available in such emergencies.)

Once I lost my favorite brooch. I spent weeks

looking everywhere for it. Finally, I gave up. Less than one day later, I found the brooch pinned on a sweater.

When I need something in my life, I trust it will be found at the right and perfect time.

Time is man-made.

A wise teacher once told me, "The past is a canceled check; the future a promissory note. The only real hard cash is in the present." Other sages preach that passion is in the moment; celebrate the temporary; take time to smell the roses. This advice is aimed at getting the human race to focus on the present.

In my life, I find myself preoccupied with the past and the future. *If only things had been different,* I think. *Maybe things will be better,* I wish. And in doing so, I am robbing myself of my only real asset—what is happening now.

Consider this: Our senses do not function in the past nor the future. We cannot see, smell, taste, hear, or feel something that has happened before or that will happen in the future. What we sense in the present may trigger a memory, but the sensation is happening in the present, not the past.

God gave us our senses as a means to experience his creation. Therefore, we are not intended to spend most of our waking hours focusing on a time when we cannot use these senses. Enjoying the sights, sounds, smells, feelings, and tastes of fall is one of the best ways we can be truly in the present and enjoy the riches of the moment.

Lord, help me stay in the present by reawakening me to the sensations I receive from the world.

You only go around once in life so why not enjoy the trip?

I am goal oriented, and I'm not alone. The majority of our society is trained from an early age to be this way. The measure of success is not how someone got to the top, but the fact that they are at the top—the end result. Being goal oriented is not bad, unless we focus so much on the goal that we miss the lessons necessary to reach that goal.

Peter Jenkins made a journey that ultimately changed his life.[4] Anyone who has read his books knows that his story does not focus on his goal—reaching the Pacific Ocean—but on the exciting and educating ventures he experienced en route. It was these interim adventures that changed his life. If the destination of his trip were more important than the journey, then he would have had no reason to write his books—and we would have no reason to read them.

For most of us the lesson is not learned at the end of the journey, but along the way. The *process* is when the magic occurs; the end result when the *applause* happens. Missing the magic and just witnessing the applause leaves us wondering what everyone is clapping about.

Today, I will enjoy the journey, the process that gets me to my goals.

The world seems so unfair because we can't see it through God's eyes.

$\mathcal{I}$ have a friend who has been stricken with cancer. She's not very old and has a young, growing family. It's a tragic set of circumstances. This woman does not possess any of the high risk factors for cancer. Until her diagnosis, she was an active, healthy individual. Even her physicians shook their heads.

I had the privilege of spending some time with my friend recently and we talked about how priorities change when one faces a life-threatening situation. "I know it sounds crazy," she told me. "While I'm not overjoyed to have this disease, I feel my life has changed for the better. My friends and family have all rallied around me and I have a new appreciation for humanity that I don't think I would have, had I not gotten cancer."

I'm not implying that God meant for this person to have cancer. I can't even comprehend what God's intentions are in this matter. And I want to shout, "It's not fair! Why does this have to happen to her? She never did anything wrong!"

Does God make mistakes? "Of course not," would be our vehement reply. But how many of us really believe it? How many of us can understand what happens in our crazy world and really feel it isn't a mistake?

The only thing I can do is accept and pray for that comprehension. If it doesn't come, at least I'm comforted in the knowledge that God is in control and he knows what he's doing.

I will try to accept my life as is (joys as well as sorrows) because I know God is in the pilot's seat and he knows how to fly this plane better than I.

> The heavens declare the glory of
> God;
> And the firmament shows His
> handiwork.
>
> —Psalm 19:1

*T*he heavens are a marvel to me. Surely, they are the finest example of God's handiwork. I spent one fall on the north shore of Lake Superior, far away from any cities. Here the night skies were breathtakingly beautiful. The stars seemed so bright, so close I could almost touch them. An added bonus was the frequent displays of northern lights. "The best in years," I was told by locals.

I was driving from Canada to Minnesota with a friend late one night when I saw my first aurora borealis. That experience remains etched in my mind. The northern lights are incredible to behold. No matter how descriptive one can be, no one knows what it's like until he or she has seen them firsthand.

My first thought upon viewing the display— pinks, purples, reds, greens—in the night sky was, *These aren't subtle at all. You can't miss the curtains of colors that fall from the heavens.* My second thought was, *It's a miracle!* And my third thought, *God can paint!*

When I look upon the night sky, I will see God's creativity in its display.

> *So Moses said to him, "As soon as*
> *I have gone out of the city, I will*
> *spread out my hands to the LORD;*
> *the thunder will cease, and there will*
> *be no more hail, that you may*
> *know that the earth is the LORD's."*
> —*Exodus 9:29*

*M*ountains surround the little town where I grew up. I remember waking up on fall mornings and seeing the mountains draped with a delicate fog that stood out against their purple-blue outlines. It happens only during the fall; the rest of the year the temperature isn't quite right for fog to form. I haven't been back to this town in years, so I don't know if the phenomenon still occurs or if there is too much smog obscuring the mountains.

My husband's grandmother lived in southern California until her death at age ninety-five. She saw a lot of changes in the Los Angeles area during her lifetime. The San Bernardino Mountains are very close to her home and she remembered being able to see them nearly every day. Not so anymore.

The global environmental crisis is hardly a surprise . . . it's a heated issue in politics and the daily news. Most of us acknowledge the world needs our help before it's too late, but we disagree who should shoulder the responsibility.

The air, soil, and water belong to the Lord and have been loaned to us while we're on the earth. We are stewards of this creation. It makes sense that we should take care of these gifts. Simply put, if we mess up our backyard, we need to clean it up or else it becomes unsafe to live in.

Cleanup doesn't have to be the responsibility of the government. A government is just a collection of people. Cleanup starts with each individual.

I will make a difference in my global environment by my individual actions today.

> *Seek in reading and thou shalt find in meditation; knock in prayer and it shall be opened to thee in contemplation.*
>
> —St. John of the Cross

*I*n the area I now live, fall is marked by dreary, rainy, gray days. Even the leaves seem to drop before their fall colors appear. It can get depressing.

Thus, I am forced to spend a lot of time indoors stoking the fire to keep dry and warm. The too-easy form of entertainment these days is the television. Fortunately (or unfortunately, depending on how I look at it), I have very limited television reception. But there's always a video to watch and, too often, my children resort to this on these rainy fall days.

When I pick up a book, however, I'm transported into a world of wonder and adventure. Reading is my passion. And I'm not alone. In fact, where I live there are more library cards per capita than anywhere else in the county.

Autumn can be a time for contemplating, a relief from the backbreaking pace of summer and its multitude of outdoor activities. One can slow down and enjoy the time indoors, nestled beneath a blanket in front of a roaring fire, safe and warm, while the weather creates havoc on the outside world.

What better time to read? Reading a good book is one of the best forms of entertainment. It is not a mindless activity like watching television or movies, which has its worth if used properly. Reading is an interactive exercise, an opportunity to join the imaginary world the author has created and to be an active participant in an adventure without ever having to leave the couch. And reading aloud to children is a special way to share.

I will read a book today. It's one of the best ways I can exercise my imagination.

> *Therefore whoever hears these sayings of Mine, and does them, I will liken him to a wise man who built his house on the rock: and the rain descended, the floods came, and the winds blew and beat on that house; and it did not fall, for it was founded on the rock.*
>
> *—Matthew 7:24–25*

*A*utumn can be a time of violent weather—a characteristic of the unstable patterns that this transitional season brings. One late autumn weekend, a disastrous flood hit the northwestern part of the United States. In a matter of hours, many people were without homes and some had lost their lives.

Since that historic event the building codes for this area have become more stringent. Building in a floodplain is almost impossible and in marginal flooding areas, very specific foundations have to be constructed to allow for the movement of floodwaters but still keep the structure anchored. Correspondingly, building costs have escalated.

Several hymns praise the foundation the Lord provides us in our own mortal lives. If we anchor our existence in his teachings and promises, if we

have faith in God, we can survive anything—
even a life-threatening catastrophe because we
know that no matter what happens to our mortal
bodies, our souls live on with God into eternity.

*I will live my life firmly anchored in
a belief in God, and that will be my
strong foundation to hold me no
matter what assails me.*

While the earth remains, seedtime and harvest, cold and heat, winter and summer, and day and night shall not cease.

—*Genesis 8:22*

*G*od's covenant with Noah was a covenant with all human beings. The evidence of this promise (in God's words) is the changing seasons. God intends us to enjoy each season as it comes and, more importantly, embrace the seasons as a natural cycle of life on earth.

As autumn nears its end and winter looms on the threshold, change is in the air. Where I live, there's an extra chill in the morning air that wasn't there before. It doesn't warm up enough during the day to melt the frost. The vegetation turns black and gray. The leaves have dropped from the trees and stark branches reach toward a slate-gray sky.

A few birds still flit about, but the outdoor activity of the animals is quieter. A stillness seems to transcend on the world. The flurry of preparation is done. The world seems poised, waiting for the coming winter and hoping it won't be too cruel.

As much as I love autumn, I look forward to winter. I know that fall can't occur year-round. I love autumn because it brings change to the world around me and because it provides contrasts in my life (vivid sensations outside, vivid memories and feelings inside). But I also love autumn because it brings winter.

I will look forward to the coming winter as a sign of God's promise to all living creatures.

NOTES

1. Brenda Ueland, *If You Want to Write* (St. Paul, MN: Graywolf Press, 1987).
2. C. S. Lewis, *The Lion, The Witch, and The Wardrobe* (New York, NY: Macmillian Publishing Company, Inc., 1978).
3. Laura Ingalls Wilder, *The Little House in the Big Woods: Little House on the Prairie* (New York, NY: Harper & Row, Publishers, 1960).
4. Peter Jenkins, *A Walk Across America II* (New York: William Morrow and Company, Inc., 1981).